A CHILD'S BOOK OF

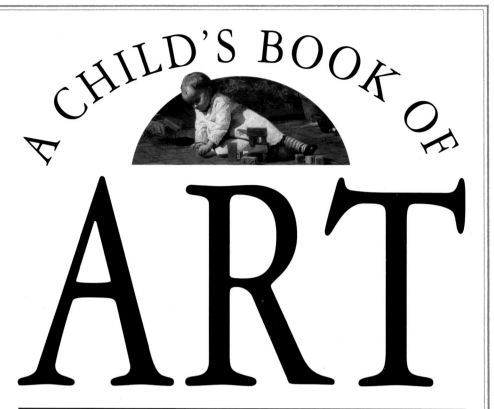

ART

GREAT PICTURES
FIRST WORDS

SELECTED BY
—— LUCY ——
MICKLETHWAIT

A DK PUBLISHING BOOK

This book is for
Walter and Molly

Editor Elizabeth Wilkinson
Designer Mary Sandberg
U.S. Editor B. Alison Weir
Picture Researcher Milly Trowbridge
Production Samantha Larmour

First American Edition, 1993

11 25 24 23 22 21

023-KB310-Nov/93

Published in the United States by
DK Publishing Inc., 375 Hudson Street
New York, New York 10014

Library of Congress Cataloging-in-Publication Data

Micklethwait, Lucy.
   A child's book of art / by Lucy Micklethwait. — 1st American ed.
      p.   cm.
   Includes index.
   Summary: An introduction to art that uses well-known works of art
to illustrate familiar words.
   ISBN-13 : 978-1-56458-203-4

   1. Art appreciation — Juvenile literature. (1. Art appreciation.
2. Vocabulary.) I. Title.
N7477.M53   1993   92-54320
701'.1—dc20   CIP
                                                                    AC

Color reproduction by CS Graphics, Singapore
Printed and bound in China by L.Rex Printing Co., Ltd.

Dorling Kindersley would like to thank the following
for their help in producing this book: Mathewson Bull,
Sheila Hanly, Richard Czapnik.

See our complete product line at
www.dk.com

Contents

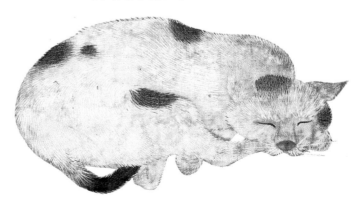

Note to Parents and Teachers

It is never too early to introduce children to art. When my children were very young, I cut pictures of paintings from magazines and pasted them onto my kitchen walls, from floor to ceiling. The most interesting I put at toddler height or within reach of the high chair. With art around the home and in the classroom, children can become familiar with it and begin to appreciate it.

Parents and teachers can have great fun learning about art with children. There is no better guide than a child, for children look at every picture with fresh eyes and honesty; they look straight into a picture to absorb what is there and they respond instinctively. To them it does not matter who a painting is by, or how important it is; the work of an Italian Master will be judged on the same terms as that of an amateur. Looking at art with children is refreshing, exciting, and often outrageously funny. As we grow older, many of us lose the ability to respond with confidence to what we see; children can help us look again with a clear eye.

Treat these pictures as you would those in any other picture book. Look for the details, talk about the colors, discuss the clothes or the weather, or talk about how the picture makes you feel. Babies may respond to highly detailed pictures with precise lines, colors, and patterns. Young children may have fun making the noises of the animals depicted or talking about the shapes and colors in an abstract painting. Older children may appreciate the use of space in a Japanese print or the feeling of springtime in an Impressionist painting.

The history of art provides endless opportunities for discussion and for expanding a child's vocabulary and general knowledge.

In choosing the pictures for this book, I relied on instinct, on my experience with illustrated books, and on the opinions of many children who, over the years, have told me what they like best. After much consideration, I decided that sculpture would lose too much of its magic on the printed page, so the works of art in this book are all two-dimensional.

A Child's Book of Art is a book to grow up with. On pages 62-64 there is additional information to enable the reader to find out more about the pictures and artists. As an introduction to the history of art, however, all we need are the pictures themselves. Just by looking at them, children can learn a great deal. They will spot different paintings by the same artist, observe the differences in style and technique, and learn to put the works of art into chronological order. The precious ability to look, and see, and think for themselves must be nurtured and encouraged. With this, children can acquire a real understanding of art. Later on, they may reach out for more information in order to increase their knowledge.

Art is rich with the magic and wisdom of centuries. By opening our children's eyes to it, we can help them understand and appreciate the world in which they live and the people with whom they share it.

The Family

The Family of Jan-Baptista Anthoine, 1664, Gonzales Coques

mother

father

children

sisters

The Calmady Children: Emily, (1818-1906)
and Laura Anne, (1820-1894), c.1823, Thomas Lawrence

The Princes in the Tower (detail),
1878, John Everett Millais

brothers

brother
and sister

John Parker and his Sister Theresa, 1779, Joshua Reynolds

At Home

in the bedroom

Bedroom at Arles, 1889, Vincent van Gogh

in the bathroom

Woman in her Bath, Sponging her Leg, 1883, Edgar Degas

in the dining room

*Portrait of William Brooke, 10th Lord Cobham
and his Family,* 1567, attributed to the
Master of the Countess of Warwick

in the kitchen

The Sleeping Kitchen Maid, 1655, Nicolaes Maes

In the Garden

A Girl with a Watering Can, 1876, Auguste Renoir

watering the plants

reading

The Garden of Paradise, c.1410, The Master of the Upper Rhine

picking fruit   playing music   fetching water

Pets

dog

Miss Jane Bowles (detail),
1775, Joshua Reynolds

rabbit

Boy and Rabbit,
exhibited 1816, Henry Raeburn

donkey

Paul on the Donkey,
1923, Pablo Picasso

kitten

A Girl with a Kitten,
1745, Jean-Baptiste Perronneau

parrot

Parrot outside his Cage, 17th century, Cornelis Biltius

Animals on the Farm

The Residence of David Twining 1787, c.1846, Edward Hicks

in the farmyard

ewe and
lamb

Cheviot Ewe and Lamb, c.1835, William Shiels

piglets

Girl with Pigs, before 1782, Thomas Gainsborough

bull and cow

Landscape with Cattle, 1895-1900, Henri Rousseau

Wild Animals

Tortoise, 17th century,
from a Turkish manuscript

tortoise

The Hare, 1502, Albrecht Dürer

hare

kangaroos
and a lizard

Kangaroos, 20th century,
detail from an Aboriginal bark painting

tiger

Tropical Storm with a Tiger, 1891, Henri Rousseau

lots of animals

The Raven Addressing the Assembled Animals, c.1590, Indian

Birds

flock
of birds

Flock of White-eyes, 1820, Satō Suiseki

cockatoo,
crane,
bullfinch,
and thrush

Indian Crane, Cockatoo, Bullfinch, and Thrush,
c.1880, Henry Stacy Marks

eagle

Eagle over Fukagawa, c.1857, Utagawa Hiroshige

geese

Two Red-breasted Geese and a Bean Goose,
c. 2550 BC, detail from an Egyptian tomb painting

Fruit

a basket of fruit

Basket of Fruit, c.1596, Caravaggio

apples, pears,
and grapes

Flowers and Fruit, 1865, Henri Fantin-Latour

plums, peaches, and cherries

Plums and Peaches,
17th century, Jacob van Hulsdonck

oranges and lemons

Still-life with Lemons, Oranges, and a Rose,
1633, Francisco de Zurbarán

Things to Do

reading

The Virgin (detail), c.1426-27,
Hubert and Jan van Eyck

writing

Woman Writing a Letter,
c.1655, Gerard ter Borch

drawing

The Artist's Son, Jean, Drawing, 1901, Auguste Renoir

painting

Portrait of the Artist, 1791,
Louise Elisabeth Vigée-Lebrun

Action Words

dancing

*A Pair of Girls with Joined Hands
Performing a Kathak Dance* (detail),
c.1675, Indian

riding

The Jockey, 1899, Henri dé Toulouse-Lautrec

swimming

Le Plongeur, 1978, David Hockney

Footrace, c.530 BC, Greek vase painting

running

swinging

The Swing, 1767, Jean-Honoré Fragonard

Counting

1

The Boy with the Fife,
1866, Edouard Manet

one boy

2

Putti from Madonna and Child with Saints,
c.1518, Rosso Fiorentino

two angels

3

three girls

Portrait of Three Young Girls, early 17th century, Circle of Robert Peake

four sisters

The Daughters of Sir Matthew Decker Bart., 1718, Jan de Meyer

5

five children

The Five Children of Charles I,
1637, Anthony van Dyck

Colors

dressed
in black

Portrait of a Girl, possibly Magdalena Luther,
c.1535, Lucas Cranach the Elder

dressed in white

Paul as Pierrot, 1925, Pablo Picasso

yellow sunflowers

Girl with Sunflowers,
1941, Diego Rivera

red room

Red Interior, Still-life on a Blue Table, 1947, Henri Matisse

More Colors

green grass

A Lawn Sprinkler, 1967, David Hockney

blue sea

Antibes, 1888, Claude Monet

Succession, 1935, Wassily Kandinsky

lots of colors

Shapes

Electric Prisms, 1914, Sonia Delaunay

circles

triangles

and squares

Composition, 1918-20, Bart van der Leck

Pompeii, 1959, Hans Hofmann

rectangles

Opposites

big and
small

Dignity and Impudence, 1839, Edwin Landseer

happy

sad

*Miniature Portraits of Two
Little Girls,* 1590, Isaac Oliver

My First Sermon, 1863, John Everett Millais

awake

My Second Sermon, 1864, John Everett Millais

asleep

young
and old

Old Man and Child,
1827, Richard Parkes Bonington

More Opposites

up

and

down

the stairs

House of Stairs 1, 1951, M. C. Escher

over and under the bridge

Evening Scene on the Occasion of the Festival of Lanterns,
c.1834, Katsushika Hokusai

The Seasons

Spring, 1886, Claude Monet

spring

summer

Wheatfield with Reaper, 1889, Vincent van Gogh

fall

Autumn Leaves, 1856, John Everett Millais

winter

The Hunters in the Snow,
1565, Pieter Bruegel the Elder

The Weather

rainy

Sudden Shower on the Ohashi Bridge.
c.1857, Utagawa Hiroshige

Winter. 1586, Lucas van Valckenborch

snowy

A High Wind at Yeigiri, c.1830-35, Katsushika Hokusai

windy

sunny

Spring Morning, c.1875, James Tissot

By the Sea

Children Playing on the Beach, 1884, Mary Cassatt

playing in the sand

July, the Seaside, 1943, L. S. Lowry

a crowded beach

A Holiday, 1915, Edward Potthast

splashing in the sea

Faces

sideways face

The Dead King Amenophis I,
c.1050 BC, detail from an
Egyptian coffin painting

mixed-up face

The Sailor, 1938, Pablo Picasso

flat face

The Brown Bear, 19th century,
detail from a ceremonial robe of
the Tlingit nation, North American

magical faces

Magical Calendar (detail), c.1300–1500, Aztec book painting

fierce face

The Kabuki Actor Nakamura
Utaemon III in the Role of a Samurai,
1825, Shunkōsai Hokushū

The Five Senses

hearing

The Listening Girl,
1780s, Jean-Baptiste Greuze

seeing

Mother and Child, c.1905, Mary Cassatt

smelling

Smell, 1637, Jan Molenaer

The Glass of Wine, c.1660, Jan Vermeer

tasting

touching

The Creation of Adam (detail), 1511, Michelangelo

Six Ways to Travel

The Diplomats, 1939, Peter Purves Smith

A Mahout Riding an Elephant (detail), 17th century, Indian

by car and

airplane

by elephant

Father Juniet's Cart, 1908, Henri Rousseau

by horse and cart

Homage to Louis David, 1948-49, Fernand Léger

by bicycle

Boston and North Chungahochie Express, after 1919, American

by train

49

Let's Go by Boat

fishing boats

Mount Fuji Seen Through a Fishing Net on a Clear Day,
c.1843, Utagawa Kuniyoshi

passenger boat

The Month of May, c.1540, Simon Benninck

The Owl and the Pussycat, 1981-83, Peter Blake

sailboat

*Scene on Lake Tana, showing people going to a festival
at an island church*, 20th century, Ethiopian

canoes

A Time to Work

farming

October, Planting Seeds, c.1415, The Limbourg Brothers

The Birth of Christ,
c.1404, Konrad von Soest

cooking

Masons Building the Wall Around the Town (detail),
15th century, from a French manuscript

building

The Country School, 1871, Winslow Homer

teaching and learning

A Time to Play

cards

The Cheat with the Ace of Diamonds, probably late 1620s, Georges de la Tour

toys

Baby at Play, 1876, Thomas Eakins

The Badminton Game, 1972-73, David Inshaw

sports

A Putto Musician, c.1520, Rosso Fiorentino

music

A Time to Eat

breakfast

Madonna Feeding the Child, c.1510-15, Gerard David

lunch

One of the Family, 1880, F. G. Cotman

dinner

The King of Portugal and John of Gaunt,
15th century, from a French manuscript

A Time to Sleep

on a wall

Man Lying on a Wall, 1957, L. S. Lowry

on a chair

Flaming June, exhibited 1895, Frederic Leighton

on a cushion

Cupid Asleep (detail),
probably 1620s, Guido Reni

on the grass

Cat Sleeping under Peonies (detail),
c.1800, Japanese hanging scroll

A Time for Peace

Peaceable Kingdom, c.1834, Edward Hicks

The wolf also shall dwell with the lamb, and the leopard shall lie down with the kid; and the calf and the young lion and the fatling together; and a little child shall lead them.

Isaiah 11:6

Picture List

The Family

6: *The Family of Jan-Baptista Anthoine,* 1664
Gonzales Coques, 1614 or 1618-1684, Flemish
oil on copper
22¼" x 29"
Royal Collection, St. James's Palace, London, England

7: *The Princes in the Tower* (detail), 1878
John Everett Millais, 1829-1896, British
oil on canvas
58" x 36"
Royal Holloway and Bedford New College, Surrey, England

7: *The Calmady Children: Emily, (1818-1906) and Laura Anne, (1820-1894),* c.1823
Thomas Lawrence, 1769-1830, British
oil on canvas
31" x 30"
Metropolitan Museum of Art, New York
Bequest of Collis P. Huntington, 1925

7: *John Parker and his Sister Theresa,* 1779
Joshua Reynolds, 1723-1792, British
oil on canvas
56" x 43¾"
National Trust, Saltram, Devon, England

At Home

8: *Bedroom at Arles,* 1889
Vincent van Gogh, 1853-1890, Dutch
oil on canvas
22" x 29"
Musée d'Orsay, Paris, France

8: *Woman in her Bath, Sponging her Leg,* 1883
Edgar Degas, 1834-1917, French
pastel on paper
8" x 16"
Musée d'Orsay, Paris, France

9: *Portrait of William Brooke, 10th Lord Cobham and his Family,* 1567
Attributed to the Master of the Countess of Warwick, working 1560-1570
oil on wood
36¼" x 47"
Longleat House, Wiltshire, England

9: *The Sleeping Kitchen Maid,* 1655
Nicolaes Maes, 1634-1693, Dutch
oil on oak
27½" x 21"
National Gallery, London, England

In the Garden

10: *A Girl with a Watering Can,* 1876
Auguste Renoir, 1841-1919, French
oil on canvas
39¼" x28¾"
National Gallery of Art, Washington, D.C.
Chester Dale Collection

11: *The Garden of Paradise,* c.1410
The Master of the Upper Rhine
tempera on wood
10¼" x 13"
Städelsches Kunstinstitut, Frankfurt, Germany

Pets

12: *Miss Jane Bowles* (detail), 1775
Joshua Reynolds, 1723-1792, British
oil on canvas
35¾" x 28"
Wallace Collection, London, England

12: *Boy and Rabbit,* exhibited 1816
Henry Raeburn, 1756-1823, British
oil on canvas
40" x 31"
Royal Academy of Arts, London, England

12: *Paul on the Donkey,* 1923
Pablo Picasso, 1881-1973, Spanish
oil on canvas
39½" x 32"
Collection Bernard Picasso, Paris, France

13: *A Girl with a Kitten,* 1745
Jean-Baptiste Perronneau, b. c.1715, d.1783, French
pastel on paper
23¼" x 19½"
National Gallery, London, England

13: *Parrot outside his Cage*
Cornelis Biltius, working 1654-1673, Dutch
oil on canvas
23¾" x 33¼"
Private Collection

Animals on the Farm

14: *The Residence of David Twining 1787,* c.1846
Edward Hicks, 1780-1849, American
oil on canvas
26½" x 31½"
Abby Aldrich Rockefeller Folk Art Center, Williamsburg, Virginia

14: *Cheviot Ewe and Lamb,* c.1835
William Shiels, 1785-1857, British
oil on canvas
39¾" x 54¼"
National Museum of Antiquities of Scotland, Edinburgh

15: *Girl with Pigs,* before 1782
Thomas Gainsborough, 1727-1788, British
oil on canvas
51" x 60"
Castle Howard Collection, Yorkshire, England

15: *Landscape with Cattle,* 1895-1900
Henri Rousseau, 1844-1910, French
oil on canvas
20" x 25½"
Philadelphia Museum of Art
Louise and Walter Arensberg Collection

Wild Animals

16: *The Hare,* 1502
Albrecht Dürer, 1471-1528, German
watercolor on paper
10" x 9"
Albertina, Vienna, Austria

16: *Tortoise,* 17th century
Illustration from a Turkish manuscript, translated from an earlier Arabic text
watercolor on paper
13" x 8" (page), 2" x 4½" (tortoise)
Jewish National and University Library, Jerusalem, Israel

16: *Kangaroos,* 20th century
Detail from an Aboriginal bark painting, Australian
natural pigments on bark
Private Collection

16: *Tropical Storm with a Tiger,* 1891
Henri Rousseau, 1844-1910, French
oil on canvas
51" x 63¾"
National Gallery, London, England

17: *The Raven Addressing the Assembled Animals,* c.1590
Illustration to a Persian Fable, Indian, Mughal School
gouache on paper
10½" x 7½"
British Museum, London, England

Birds

18: *Flock of White-eyes,* from the picture album *Suiseki Gafu Nihen,* 1820
Satō Suiseki, working c.1806-1840, Japanese
color-printed from woodblocks
10" x 7" (each page) 9½" x 5½" (each image shown)
British Museum, London, England

18: *Indian Crane, Cockatoo, Bullfinch, and Thrush,* c.1880
Henry Stacy Marks, 1829-1898, British
oil on canvas
48" x 32"
Private Collection

19: *Eagle over Fukagawa,* from the series *One Hundred Views of Edo,* c.1857
Utagawa Hiroshige, 1797-1858, Japanese
color print from woodblocks
14" x 9¼"
British Museum, London, England

19: *Two Red-breasted Geese and a Bean Goose,* c.2550 BC
Detail from a frieze from the tomb chapel of Itet at Meidum, 4th Dynasty, Egyptian
paint on plaster
Height approx. 9½" (detail shown)
Egyptian Museum, Cairo, Egypt

Fruit

20: *Basket of Fruit,* c.1596
Caravaggio (real name: Michelangelo Merisi), 1573-1610, Italian
oil on canvas
18" x 25¼"
Pinacoteca Ambrosiana, Milan, Italy

20: *Flowers and Fruit,* 1865
Henri Fantin-Latour, 1836-1904, French
oil on canvas
25" x 22½"
Musée d'Orsay, Paris, France

21: *Plums and Peaches*
Jacob van Hulsdonck, 1582-1647, Flemish
oil on copper
11¼" x 13¾"
Private Collection

21: *Still-life with Lemons, Oranges, and a Rose,* 1633
Francisco de Zurbarán, 1598-1664, Spanish
oil on canvas
24¼" x 43"
Norton Simon Museum, Pasadena, California

Things to Do

22: *The Virgin* (detail), c.1426-27, from *The Ghent Polyptych*
Hubert van Eyck, d.c.1426, and Jan van Eyck, working 1422, d.1441, Netherlandish
oil on wood
66½" x 29½"
Cathedral of St. Bavo, Ghent, Belgium

23: *Woman Writing a Letter,* c.1655
Gerard ter Borch, 1617-1681, Dutch
oil on wood
15½" x 11½"
Mauritshuis, The Hague, the Netherlands

23: *The Artist's Son, Jean, Drawing,* 1901
Auguste Renoir, 1841-1919, French
oil on canvas
17¾" x 21½"
Virginia Museum of Fine Arts, Richmond
Collection of Mr. and Mrs. Paul Mellon

23: *Portrait of the Artist,* 1791
Louise Elisabeth Vigée-Lebrun, 1755-1842, French
oil on canvas
39" x 31¾"
National Trust, Ickworth, Suffolk, England

Action Words

24: *A Pair of Girls with Joined Hands Performing a Kathak Dance* (detail), c.1675
Indian, Mughal School
gouache on paper
8¾" x 5½"
Victoria and Albert Museum, London, England

24: *The Jockey,* 1899
Henri de Toulouse-Lautrec, 1864-1901, French
color lithograph
20¼" x 14¼"
National Gallery of Victoria, Melbourne
Australia, Felton Bequest

24: *Le Plongeur,* No.18 of *Paper Pools* series, 1978
David Hockney, b.1937, British
paint and molded paper pulp
72" x 14' 3"
Hockney Gallery, Saltaire, Bradford, England
On loan from Bradford Art Galleries and Museums

25: *Footrace,* c.530 BC
Detail from a black-figured prize amphora, attributed to the Euphiletos Painter, Greek
terracotta
Height of amphora 24½"
Metropolitan Museum of Art, New York
Rogers Fund 1914

25: *The Swing,* 1767
Jean-Honoré Fragonard, 1732-1806, French
oil on canvas
32¾" x 26"
Wallace Collection, London, England

Counting

26: *The Boy with the Fife,* 1866
Edouard Manet, 1832-1883, French
oil on canvas
64½" x 38¼"
Musée d'Orsay, Paris, France

26: *Putti,* detail from *Madonna and Child with Saints,* c.1518
Rosso Fiorentino, 1494-1540, Italian
oil on wood
67¾" x 55½"
Uffizi Gallery, Florence, Italy

26: *Portrait of Three Young Girls*
Circle of Robert Peake, working 1598, d. c.1626, British
oil on wood
33½" x 46"
Private Collection

27: *The Daughters of Sir Matthew Decker Bart.,* 1718
Jan de Meyer, b.before 1696, d.after 1740, Dutch
oil on canvas
30½" x 26"
Fitzwilliam Museum, Cambridge, England

27: *The Five Children of Charles I,* 1637
Anthony van Dyck, 1599-1641, Flemish
oil on canvas
64¼" x 78¼"
Royal Collection, St. James's Palace, London, England

Colors

28: *Portrait of a Girl, possibly Magdalena Luther,* c.1535
Lucas Cranach the Elder, 1472-1553, German
oil on wood
16¼" x 10¼"
Musée du Louvre, Paris, France

28: *Paul as Pierrot,* 1925
Pablo Picasso, 1881-1973, Spanish
oil on canvas
51¼" x 38¼"
Musée Picasso, Paris, France

28: *Girl with Sunflowers,* 1941
Diego Rivera, 1886-1957, Mexican
oil on canvas
36½" x 29¼"
Private Collection

29: *Red Interior, Still-life on a Blue Table,* 1947
Henri Matisse, 1869-1954, French
oil on canvas
45¾" x 35"
Kunstsammlung Nordrhein-Westfalen, Düsseldorf, Germany

More Colors

30: *A Lawn Sprinkler,* 1967
David Hockney, b.1937, British
acrylic on canvas
48" x 48"
Private Collection

31: *Antibes,* 1888
Claude Monet, 1840-1926, French
oil on canvas
25¾" x 36½"
Courtauld Institute Galleries, London, England

31: *Succession,* 1935
Wassily Kandinsky, 1866-1944, Russian
oil on canvas
31" x 39"
Phillips Collection, Washington, D.C.

Shapes

32: *Electric Prisms,* 1914
Sonia Delaunay, 1885-1979, b.Russia, lived in France from 1905
oil on canvas
98½" x 98½"
Musée National d'Art Moderne, Paris, France

32: *Composition,* 1918-20
Bart van der Leck, 1876-1958, Dutch
oil on canvas
39¾" x 39½"
Stedelijk Museum, Amsterdam, the Netherlands

33: *Pompeii,* 1959
Hans Hofmann, 1880-1966, b.Germany, American citizen from 1941
oil on canvas
84½" x 52"
Tate Gallery, London, England

Opposites

34: *Dignity and Impudence,* 1839
Edwin Landseer, 1803-1873, British
oil on canvas
35" x 27¼"
Tate Gallery, London, England

34: *Miniature Portraits of Two Little Girls,* 1590
Isaac Oliver, d.1617, b.France, lived in England
bodycolor on vellum mounted on card
2" x 1¼"
Victoria and Albert Museum, London, England

35: *My First Sermon,* 1863
John Everett Millais, 1829-1896, British
oil on canvas
36¼" x 30¼"
Guildhall Art Gallery, Corporation of London, England

35: *My Second Sermon,* 1864
John Everett Millais, 1829-1896, British
oil on canvas
38¼" x 28¼"
Guildhall Art Gallery, Corporation of London, England

35: *Old Man and Child,* 1827
Richard Parkes Bonington, 1802-1828, British
watercolor on paper
7½" x 5½"
Wallace Collection, London, England

More Opposites

36: *House of Stairs 1,* 1951
M. C. Escher, 1898-1972, Dutch
lithograph
18½" x 9½"
Gemeentemuseum, The Hague, the Netherlands

37: *Evening Scene on the Occasion of the Festival of Lanterns,* from the series *Splendid Views of Famous Bridges of the Provinces,* c.1834
Katsushika Hokusai, 1760-1849, Japanese
color print from woodblocks
10" x 15"
Victoria and Albert Museum, London, England

The Seasons

38: *Spring,* 1886
Claude Monet, 1840-1926, French
oil on canvas
25½" x 31¾"
Fitzwilliam Museum, Cambridge, England

38: *Wheatfield with Reaper,* 1889
Vincent van Gogh, 1853-1890, Dutch
oil on canvas
29" x 36¼"
Van Gogh Museum, Amsterdam, the Netherlands

39: *Autumn Leaves,* 1856
John Everett Millais, 1829-1896, British
oil on canvas
41" x 29"
City Art Gallery, Manchester, England

39: *The Hunters in the Snow,* 1565
Pieter Bruegel the Elder, b.c.1525/30, d.1569, Netherlandish
oil on wood
46" x 63¾"
Kunsthistorisches Museum, Vienna, Austria

The Weather

40: *Sudden Shower on the Ohashi Bridge,* from the series *One Hundred Views of Edo,* c.1857
Utagawa Hiroshige, 1797-1858, Japanese
color print from woodblocks
13¼" x 8¾"
Whitworth Art Gallery, Manchester, England

40: *Winter,* 1586
Lucas van Valckenborch, c.1530-1597, Netherlandish
oil on canvas
46" x 78"
Kunsthistorisches Museum, Vienna, Austria

41: *A High Wind at Yeigiri,* from the series *Thirty-six Views of Mount Fuji,* c.1830-35
Katsushika Hokusai, 1760-1849, Japanese
color print from woodblocks
10¼" x 15"
British Museum, London, England

41: *Spring Morning,* c.1875
James Tissot, 1836-1902, French
oil on canvas
24½" x 16"
Private Collection

By the Sea

42: *Children Playing on the Beach,* 1884
Mary Cassatt, 1844-1926, American
oil on canvas
38¼" x 29¼"
National Gallery of Art, Washington, D.C.
Ailsa Mellon Bruce Collection

43: *July, the Seaside,* 1943
L. S. Lowry, 1887-1976, British
oil on canvas
26¼" x 36½"
Arts Council Collection, London, England

43: *A Holiday,* 1915
Edward Potthast, 1857-1927, American
oil on canvas
30½" x 40½"
Art Institute of Chicago, Illinois
Friends of American Art Collection

Faces

44: *The Dead King Amenophis I,* patron of the Theban workmen, c.1050 BC
Detail from the floor of the coffin of the Theban official Ahmose, 21st Dynasty, Egyptian
paint on wood
approx. 15¾" x 11¼" (detail shown)
British Museum, London, England

44: *The Sailor,* 1938
Pablo Picasso, 1881-1973, Spanish
oil on canvas
23½" x 19¾"
National Gallery, London, England
Berggruen Collection

44: *The Brown Bear,* 19th century
Detail from a ceremonial robe of the Tlingit nation, North American
cloth woven from mountain goat wool
approx. 5" x 6" (detail shown)
Portland Art Museum, Oregon

45: Detail from the *Magical Calendar* of *Codex Cospi,* one of the sacred painted books of Ancient Mexico, c.1300-1500
Aztec
natural pigments on deer skin
approx. 7" x 7" (section), 12' (total length)
Biblioteca Universitaria, Bologna, Italy

45: *The Kabuki Actor Nakamura Utaemon III in the Role of a Samurai,* from the series *Famous Roles of Utaemon,* 1825
Shunkōsai Hokushū, working 1808-1832, Japanese
color print from woodblocks
10" x 14½"
Victoria and Albert Museum, London, England

The Five Senses

46: *Mother and Child,* c.1905
Mary Cassatt, 1844-1926, American
oil on canvas
36¼" x 29"
National Gallery of Art, Washington, D.C.
Chester Dale Collection

46: *The Listening Girl,* 1780s
Jean-Baptiste Greuze, 1725-1805, French
oil on mahogany
19" x 15½"
Wallace Collection, London, England

46: *Smell,* from the series *The Five Senses,* 1637
Jan Molenaer, b. c.1610, d.1668, Dutch
oil on mahogany
7¾" x 9½"
Mauritshuis, The Hague, the Netherlands

47: *The Glass of Wine,* c.1660
Jan Vermeer, 1632-1675, Dutch
oil on canvas
26" x 30"
Gemäldegalerie, Staatliche Museum, Berlin, Germany

47: *The Creation of Adam* (detail), 1511, from the ceiling of the Sistine Chapel
Michelangelo Buonarroti, 1475-1564, Italian fresco
approx. 9' 2" x 18' 7"
Vatican, Rome, Italy

Six Ways to Travel

48: *The Diplomats,* 1939
Peter Purves Smith, 1912-1949, Australian
oil on canvas
16" x 20"
National Gallery of Australia, Canberra
Gift of Lady Casey, 1979

48: *A Mahout Riding an Elephant* (detail), 17th century
Indian, Mughal School
tinted drawing on paper
10½" x 7¼"
Victoria and Albert Museum, London, England

48: *Father Juniet's Cart,* 1908
Henri Rousseau, 1844-1910, French
oil on canvas
38¼" x 50¾"
Musée de l'Orangerie, Paris, France

49: *Homage to Louis David,* 1948-49
Fernand Léger, 1881-1955, French
oil on canvas
60½" x 73"
Musée National d'Art Moderne, Paris, France

49: *Boston and North Chungahochie Express,* after 1919
American
oil or tempera on composition board
18½" x 24½"
National Gallery of Art, Washington, D.C.
Gift of Edgar William and Bernice Chrysler Garbisch

Let's Go by Boat

50: *Mount Fuji Seen Through a Fishing Net on a Clear Day,* from the series *Thirty-six Views of Mount Fuji from Edo,* c.1843
Utagawa Kuniyoshi, 1797-1861, Japanese
color print from woodblocks
9" x 13¾"
Victoria and Albert Museum, London, England

50: *The Month of May,* a leaf from the calendar of an illuminated Book of Hours, c.1540
Simon Benninck, 1483-1561, Netherlandish
bodycolor on vellum
5½" x 3¾"
Victoria and Albert Museum, London, England

51: *The Owl and the Pussycat,* 1981-83
Peter Blake, b.1932, British
oil on hardboard
10¾" x 12½"
City of Bristol Museum and Art Gallery, England

51: *Scene on Lake Tana, showing people going to a festival at an island church,* 20th century
Ethiopian
gouache on cloth
29½" x 43¼"
Horniman Museum, London, England

A Time to Work

52: *October, Planting Seeds,* c. 1415, from the calendar of the illuminated Book of Hours *Les Très Riches Heures du Duc de Berry*
The Limbourg Brothers, working 1401-16, Netherlandish
paint on vellum
11½" x 8¾" (page) 9" x 5½" (image shown)
Musée Condé, Chantilly, France

53: *The Birth of Christ,* c.1404, a scene from the Wildunger Altarpiece
Konrad von Soest, b. early 1370s, German
tempera and gold on wood
29" x 22"
St. Nikolaus Church, Nieder-Wildungen, Bad Wildungen, Germany

53: Detail from *Masons Building the Wall Around the Town,* illustration to *City of Women,* from the *Collected Works of Christine de Pisan,* 15th century
Illuminated manuscript, French
paint on vellum
14" x 11" (page), 4" x 3¾" (detail shown)
British Library, London, England

53: *The Country School,* 1871
Winslow Homer, 1836-1910, American
oil on canvas
21¼" x 38¼"
Saint Louis Art Museum, Missouri

A Time to Play

54: *The Cheat with the Ace of Diamonds,* probably late 1620s
Georges de la Tour, 1593-1652, French
oil on canvas
41¾" x 57½"
Musée du Louvre, Paris, France

54: *Baby at Play,* 1876
Thomas Eakins, 1844-1916, American
oil on canvas
32¼" x 48¼"
National Gallery of Art, Washington, D.C.
John Hay Whitney Collection

55: *The Badminton Game,* 1972-73
David Inshaw, b.1943, British
oil on canvas
60" x 72¼"
Tate Gallery, London, England

55: *A Putto Musician,* c.1520
Rosso Fiorentino, 1494-1540, Italian
oil on wood
15¼" x 18½"
Uffizi Gallery, Florence, Italy

A Time to Eat

56: *Madonna Feeding the Child,* c.1510-15
Gerard David, working 1485, d.1523, Netherlandish
oil on oak
13¾" x 11½"
Musées Royaux des Beaux-Arts de Belgique, Brussels, Belgium

56: *One of the Family,* 1880
F. G. Cotman, 1850-1920, British
oil on canvas
40½" x 67"
Walker Art Gallery, Liverpool, England

57: *The King of Portugal and John of Gaunt,* illustration from *Chronicles of England,* Volume 3 by Jean de Wavrin, 15th century
Illuminated manuscript, French
paint on vellum
approx. 18" x 13" (page) 5½" x 8" (image shown)
British Library, London, England

A Time to Sleep

58: *Man Lying on a Wall,* 1957
L. S. Lowry, 1887-1976, British
oil on canvas
16" x 20"
City of Salford Museums and Art Gallery, England

58: *Flaming June,* exhibited 1895
Frederic Leighton, 1830-1896, British
oil on canvas
47½" x 47½"
Museo de Arte de Ponce, Puerto Rico

59: *Cupid Asleep* (detail), probably 1620s
Guido Reni, 1575-1642, Italian
oil on canvas
41½" x 54½"
Private Collection

59: *Cat Sleeping under Peonies* (detail), c.1800
Hanging scroll, Japanese
ink and colors on silk
18" x 25½"
British Museum, London, England

A Time for Peace

60: *Peaceable Kingdom,* c.1834
Edward Hicks, 1780-1849, American
oil on canvas
30" x 35½"
National Gallery of Art, Washington, D.C.
Gift of Edgar William and Bernice Chrysler Garbisch

Front Cover

From top left; clockwise:
Tropical Storm with a Tiger, page 16
The Dead King Amenophis I (detail), page 44
Bedroom at Arles, page 8
Tortoise, page 16
Miniature Portraits of Two Little Girls, page 34
Children Playing on the Beach (detail), page 42
The Artist's Son, Jean, Drawing (detail), page 23
Sudden Shower on the Ohashi Bridge, page 40
Miniature Portraits of Two Little Girls, page 34
Center
Baby at Play (detail), page 54

Front Flap

Baby at Play (detail), page 54
The Raven Addressing the Assembled Animals (detail), page 17

Back Cover

From top left; clockwise
Tropical Storm with a Tiger, page 16
Cat Sleeping under Peonies (detail), page 59
Plums and Peaches, page 21
Tortoise (detail), page 16
Children Playing on the Beach, page 42
Boston and North Chungahochie Express (detail), page 49
Spring Morning, page 41
Sudden Shower on the Ohashi Bridge, page 40
Center
Baby at Play (detail), page 54

Title Page

Baby at Play (detail), page 54
Le Plongeur, page 24

Contents

The Family of Jan-Baptista Anthoine, page 6
The Hare (detail), page 16
Plums and Peaches (detail), page 21
Putti, detail from *Madonna and Child with Saints*, page 26
Miniature Portraits of Two Little Girls, page 34
Winter, page 40
The Listening Girl, page 46
The Cheat with the Ace of Diamonds, page 54
Cat Sleeping under Peonies (detail), page 59

Note to Parents and Teachers

The Jockey, page 24
A Pair of Girls with Joined Hands Performing a Kathak Dance (detail), page 24
Indian Crane, Cockatoo, Bullfinch, and Thrush, page 18
Tortoise (detail), page 16
The Dead King Amenophis I (detail), page 44
Cupid Asleep (detail), page 59
Eagle over Fukagawa, page 19
The Virgin (detail), page 22
Boston and North Chungahochie Express, page 49

The author and publisher would like to thank the museums, galleries, and collectors listed for their kind permission to reproduce the pictures in this book.

Acknowledgments

The author and publisher would like to thank the following for their permission to reproduce copyright material:

pages 6-7
Coques: © HM the Queen
Millais: photo Bridgeman Art Library
Lawrence: © 1992 by the Metropolitan Museum of Art
Reynolds: © The National Trust 1991
pages 8-9
Van Gogh: © photo RMN
Degas: © photo RMN
att. to Master of the Countess of Warwick: reproduced by permission of the Marquess of Bath
pages 10-11
Renoir: © 1992 National Gallery of Art, Washington
Master of the Upper Rhine: photo Artothek
pages 12-13
Reynolds: Trustees of the Wallace Collection
Picasso: © DACS 1993 / Colorphoto Hans Hinz
Biltius: photo Bridgeman Art Library / Rafael Valls Gallery, London
pages 14-15
Shiels: © the Trustees of the National Museums of Scotland 1993
pages 16-17
Dürer: Graphische Sammlung Albertina, Vienna
Aboriginal bark painting: photo Werner Forman Archive
pages 18-19
H.S. Marks: photo Bridgeman Art Library
Egyptian Geese: photo Werner Forman Archive
pages 20-21
Caravaggio: photo SCALA
Fantin-Latour: © photo RMN
Van Hulsdonck: photo Christies
De Zurbarán: The Norton Simon Foundation F. 1972. 6. P.
pages 22-23
Van Eyck, Hubert and Jan: photo Giraudon / Bridgeman Art Library
Ter Borch: © Mauritshuis, The Hague, inv.Nr. 797
Vigée-Lebrun: © The National Trust 1991
pages 24-25
Hockney: © D. Hockney / photo Bridgeman Art Library
Greek amphora: © 1993 by the Metropolitan Museum of Art
Fragonard: Trustees of the Wallace Collection
pages 26-27
Manet: © photo RMN
Fiorentino: photo SCALA
Circle of Robert Peake: photo Sotheby's
Van Dyck: © HM the Queen
pages 28-29
Cranach: © photo RMN
Picasso: © DACS 1993 / © photo RMN
Rivera: reproducción autorizada por el Instituto National de Bellas Artes y Literatura / photo © Christies
Matisse: © Succession H. Matisse / DACS 1993
pages 30-31
Hockney: © D. Hockney / photo Tradhart
pages 32-33
Delaunay: © ADAGP, Paris and DACS, London 1993
Van der Leck: © DACS 1993
Hofmann: © Estate of Hans Hofmann
pages 34-35
Millais (both paintings): photos Bridgeman Art Library
Bonington: Trustees of the Wallace Collection
pages 36-37
Escher: © 1951 M.C. Escher / Cordon Art-Baarn-Holland
pages 38-39
Van Gogh: Vincent van Gogh Foundation / Van Goqh Museum, Amsterdam
pages 40-41
Tissot: photo Sotheby's
pages 42-43
Cassatt: © 1992 National Gallery of Art, Washington
Lowry: reproduced by courtesy of Mrs. Carol Ann Danes
Potthast: Friends of American Art Collection, 1915.560, photograph © 1992, The Art Institute of Chicago. All Rights Reserved.
pages 44-45
Picasso: © DACS 1993
Tlingit ceremonial robe: photo Werner Forman Archive
Magical Calendar: photo Werner Forman Archive
pages 46-47
Greuze: Trustees of the Wallace Collection
Molenaer: Photograph © Mauritshuis, The Hague
Vermeer: Photo Jörg P. Anders © BPK, Berlin 1992
Michelangelo: Photo © Nippon Television Network Corporation Tokyo 1992
pages 48-49
Rousseau: © photo RMN
Léger: © DACS 1993
Anon. American painting: © 1992 National Gallery of Art, Washington / photo by José A. Naranjo
pages 50-51
Blake: © Peter Blake / photo Bridgeman Art Library
pages 52-53:
Limbourg Brothers: photo Giraudon / Bridgeman Art Library
Konrad von Soest: photo Bridgeman Art Library
pages 54-55
De la Tour: © photo RMN
Eakins: © 1992 National Gallery of Art, Washington
Fiorentino: photo Bridgeman Art Library
pages 56-57
Cotman: The Board of Trustees of the National Museums and Galleries on Merseyside
French MS: photo Bridgeman Art Library
pages 58-59
Leighton: photo Bridgeman Art Library / Maas Gallery, London
Reni: photo Christies
pages 60-61
Hicks: © 1992 National Gallery of Art, Washington

Every effort has been made to trace the owners of copyright material, but we take this opportunity to apologize to any owners whose rights may have been unwittingly infringed.